P9-DMS-590

A Life God Rewards for Teens

Bruce Wilkinson

with David Kopp

Multnomah® Publishers *Sisters, Oregon*

A LIFE GOD REWARDS FOR TEENS
published by Multnomah Publishers, Inc.
© 2002 by Exponential, Inc.

International Standard Book Number: 1-59052-077-7

Scripture is from *The Holy Bible,* New King James Version.
Copyright © 1982 by Thomas Nelson, Inc. Used by permission.

Other Scripture quotations:

The Holy Bible, New International Version (NIV)
© 1973, 1984 by International Bible Society,
used by permission of Zondervan Publishing House

The Living Bible (TLB) © 1971. Used by permission of
Tyndale House Publishers, Inc. All rights reserved.

Multnomah is a trademark of Multnomah Publishers, Inc.,
and is registered in the U.S. Patent and Trademark Office.
The colophon is a trademark of Multnomah Publishers, Inc.

Printed in the United States of America

ALL RIGHTS RESERVED
No part of this publication may be reproduced, stored in a retrieval system,
or transmitted, in any form or by any means—electronic, mechanical,
photocopying, recording, or otherwise—without prior written permission.

For information:
MULTNOMAH PUBLISHERS, INC. • P.O. BOX 1720 • SISTERS, OREGON 97759

Library of Congress Cataloging-in-Publication Data:

Wilkinson, Bruce.
    A life God rewards for teens / by Bruce Wilkinson with David Kopp.
        p. cm.
    ISBN 1-59052-077-7
    1. Christian teenagers—Religious life.   I. Kopp, David, 1949-   II. Title.
    BV4531.3 .W55 2002
    248.3—dc21
                                                        2002015092
            02 03 04 05 06 07 08—8 7 6 5 4 3 2 1 0

TABLE OF CONTENTS

REJOICE IN THAT DAY AND
LEAP FOR **JOY** FOR INDEED
YOUR **REWARD**
IS GREAT IN
HEAVEN

JESUS, IN LUKE 6:2

a billion years
from now

You've heard the stories.

An apple falls out of a tree, and Isaac Newton starts noodling on the law of gravity. Centuries later, scientists use Newton's noodling to aim rockets at the moon.

Some Aztec warrior accidentally drops his dried-out cob of corn into the fire and *pfut, pop, pow!* Next thing you know we have popcorn by the bucket, fake butter on tap, and movies on the big screen.

Interesting, isn't it, how one little thing you do now can cause a huge thing later?

So what if I told you that who you sit next to at lunch today could change what happens to you *a billion years* from now?

I'm serious.

You decide to sit next to Eddie, one thing happens. You decide to sit next to Sam, and another thing happens…a billion years later.

And what if I told you that what happens to you then *as a direct result* of what you did today *will matter to you a lot?*

Would you be surprised? Would you think I was crazy?

The book you're holding is going to show you a big idea right in front of you that you might have missed—how your actions today can radically change your life in eternity.

This is not a book about heaven, or about how to get there, even though we'll talk about all those things and more. *A Life God Rewards for Teens* is about how to make the most of your life right now, one little opportunity at a time.

Because the honest truth is that your life today—the one-and-only life you have—is more valuable and more important and more packed with possibilities than you ever dreamed.

How Many Stars Can You See?

Let me warn you, 95 percent of the world's people believe just the opposite of what you are going to learn in the next few pages. In fact, the truths I want to show you are the exact opposite of what I believed when I first stumbled onto them. (And I had been going to church all my life.)

What you'll discover here comes from one source—the greatest teacher who ever lived. His name is Jesus. He's the only person in history who came from eternity to tell us what it is like, and what our lives on Planet Earth are meant to add up to a billion years from now. And since Jesus is the Son of God, He's the best person to tell us about God's amazing plan. That's why you'll see His name on nearly every page.

If you're willing to be surprised by the truths He revealed, it will be like seeing whole galaxies where you once saw only a tiny patch of stars.

Are you ready?

There's a big idea right in front of you that you might have missed...

Jesus Said What?

No one said more shocking things about how to live than Jesus. His words left experts outraged and ordinary people with their mouths hanging open. Take Jesus' first public appearance (He was only twelve). The Bible says, "All who heard Him were astonished at His understanding and answers" (Luke 2:47).

I'll admit, I was astonished too when I finally understood what Jesus was really saying in the Sermon on the Mount. You might be familiar with the passage:

> "Blessed are you when men hate you,
>   And when they exclude you,
> And revile you, and cast out your name as evil,
>   For the Son of Man's sake.
> Rejoice in that day and leap for joy!"
>
> LUKE 6:22–23

For years I thought Jesus meant we should *enjoy* suffering for Him. Sure. So if someone spits on you because you're a Christian, you should jump for joy because someone else's spit on your shirt makes you feel so happy.

But that never made much sense.

Then one day I read further and saw what Jesus was really saying:

"For indeed your reward is great in heaven."

v. 23

Jesus *isn't* asking you to love being miserable. Instead, He is revealing a most surprising fact.

Here it is: Do something for Jesus now, and He will do something for you later. Serve Jesus on earth, and He will reward you in heaven. And His reward for you in heaven will be so amazingly wonderful that *if you saw your future like He sees your future…* well, you might even jump for joy right now, soggy shirt and all.

Let me ask you: Do you believe that what you do for God today, in your town, with your friends, will even matter to you after you're dead?

How you answer this question says a lot about

what you think is important, how you feel about God, whether you think life is fair, and how you treat your friends (*and* your enemies).

In fact, the whole idea of a God who rewards you in heaven for what you do on earth just might be the most outrageous teaching of Jesus you ever tangle with—*especially if you're already a Christian!*

Let me show you what I mean.

My Big U-Turn

When I first saw what Jesus said about the connection between my actions now and my experience in heaven, I was upset. In fact, I told my wife that I disagreed with God's plan completely!

You see, I'd always been taught that all that mattered to God was that I receive Jesus as my Savior. If I believed the right thing, my future was guaranteed. Only people with the wrong beliefs worried about doing good works. I had my ticket to heaven—I was in. Hallelujah. End of story.

God wants to bless

So why did Jesus talk again and again about God's promise to reward people for good works?

I began a big research project, starting with every Bible verse on the subject. Then I studied what the scholars said. The more I studied, the more I noticed that our good works on earth *do* matter to God.

Jesus said He will *"reward* each according to his works"* (Matthew 16:27). And He told a wealthy person to "sell what you have and give to the poor, and you will have *treasure* in heaven" (Matthew 19:21). Obviously, Jesus wanted us to know that serving God on earth has a direct and very positive result in heaven.

Could it be, I wondered, *that the reason a lot of Christians I know don't live any differently from non-Christians is that they don't know what Jesus said about rewards?*

Gradually I realized that I had completely missed

OU—and bless you indeed—
for all eternity

what Jesus really said. I had been trying to see a million stars through a keyhole…

I decided I would make a big U-turn in my beliefs. From now on, I would believe what Jesus said, not what I thought He should say. And I would live each day as if everything I do today *will* matter forever.

Rumors of Blue Whales

That was nearly twenty years ago. I've never looked back, and my life has never been the same. And by the time you're done reading this book, if you believe the words of Jesus, your life probably will never be the same either.

You'll feel differently about people you meet every day.

You'll see awesome opportunities (with your name written all over them) on the most ordinary of days.

You'll stumble on adventures in eternity just waiting to happen *now*—in how you use your time, your money, and your abilities.

Sound like hype to you? Let me tell you, Jesus came to earth to shock people with just this kind of good news.

I promise that you'll look back on the hour or two you spent reading this book, and like Newton the Noodler, you'll think, *That's when the apple fell out of the tree…!* Or like that surprised Aztec, you'll remember, *That's when that old cob of corn suddenly started popping like crazy…!* And you'll know that the "one little thing" of reading this book has created a huge change in your life.

If you've read *The Prayer of Jabez for Teens* and *Secrets of the Vine,* you know that God wants you to ask every day for His blessing. And you know that He wants you to bear a great deal of fruit for His kingdom.

In this book you're going to see what Jesus said about how you can change your life today in ways that will change your life *forever!* You see, God wants to bless you—and bless you *indeed*—for all eternity. That's just how awesome and loving your God is!

Let's be honest, all this talk about eternity leaves us feeling small, humbled, really *human*. We're just ordinary people, stuck on the ground. We're like tadpoles swapping stories of blue whales. But God sent His Son, Jesus, from heaven to help us see huge truths we couldn't see or even imagine on our own, and to show us how to make the most of every minute of our lives.

Friend, if you're willing to be surprised, even shocked, by Jesus' words, your life can begin to change for the better immediately.

Let's Talk about It

1. Have you ever been surprised by something Jesus said? If so, what was it?

2. Do you ever feel like there's no point in trying hard to do the right thing, since Jesus will forgive you and you're going to heaven anyway? How might this affect your relationship with Jesus?

3. What comes to mind when you think about heaven? Do you think it will be the same for everyone? Why or why not?

4. Are you content with your walk with God right now, or would you like to make some big changes? How do you wish things were different?

5. If you firmly believed that everything you do today will matter greatly to you in heaven, what would you change right away?

OR INDEED YOUR
REWARD
IS GREAT IN HEAVEN

FOR THE **SON OF MAN** WILL
COME IN THE **GLORY** OF HIS
FATHER WITH HIS ANGELS

AND THEN HE WILL **REWARD**

EACH ACCORDING TO HIS WORKS

JESUS, IN MATTHEW 16:27

the truth about your (real) future

I read once that looking at the stars through a telescope from earth is a little like looking up at your brother from the bottom of a swimming pool. No matter how hard you squint, he looks pretty blurry. (I always thought my brother Gordon was better looking from the bottom of a pool.)

A telescope looks up through a vast ocean of atmosphere, so light rays from outer space look blurred and wobbly. Now you know why stars twinkle.

And now you know why astronomers were so excited when, in 1990, they launched the Hubble Space Telescope. Hubble, which is the size of a school bus, studies the stars from an orbit *above* Earth's atmosphere. No blur. No wobble. No twinkle. Almost every week, scientists are making new discoveries far out on the edges of time and space.

What if you could see your life like that?

I mean, what if you could clearly see the results of a choice you make today from a no-wobble viewpoint far out into your future?

Well, you'd probably make very *different* choices. You would know what interests and abilities you'll use most to make a living later—and you'd put more into them now. You would know which exciting invitations will turn into terrible traps later. You might even treat that really annoying person in your history class a little better (since you'd know that he or she is the person you'll fall in love with and marry years from now).

Unfortunately, you and I can't see into the future…

You would know which exciting invitations now will turn into terrible traps later.

But Someone can.

His name is Jesus. He can see the whole truth—past, present, and future. He can see your present (there you are, reading *A Life God Rewards for Teens*) from a moment far out in your infinite future and tell you exactly how to prepare for what is to come.

This chapter has one simple but extremely important purpose: *to show you the future Jesus talked about so you know what to do now.*

The (Real) Timeline of Your Eternity

Most teenagers I've met think that life happens in three stages:

- Stage One: You live on earth. *A lot of things happen.*
- Stage Two: You die. *One thing happens.*
- Stage Three: You exist in eternity. *Nothing ever happens.*

But Jesus came to tell us something very different. He revealed that, actually, most of our life happens *after* our physical death, and—guess what?—it's meant to be the *best* part of life too!

One day Jesus told His disciples about several important events that will happen in everyone's future. Listen to what He said:

> "For the Son of Man will come in the glory of His Father with His angels, and then He will reward each according to his works."
>
> MATTHEW 16:27

Do you see what Jesus is revealing in this verse? At some time in the future, Jesus will return, He will reward (or not reward) everyone, and His rewards will be based on each one's works. That's a lot of activity still to come, isn't it? And as you're about to see, that's just the beginning.

Here is a summary of the future—yours and mine—that Jesus talked about:

The Six Main Events of Your Forever Life

1. Life. You are created in the image of God for a life of purpose.

   Let's start with now. According to the Bible, you

didn't exist in the past—that rules out a previous life as, say, a lizard or a princess. Between birth and death, you live on earth as a body, soul, and spirit.

2. Death. You die physically, but not spiritually. When you die, your body returns to dust. But you are more than physical matter, and Jesus talked often about the eternal life of every person. Reincarnation isn't taught in the Bible, so you live only once…and you're always the same person.

3. Destination. You reach your eternal home after death, which is determined by what you believed on earth.

   Your eternal destination is decided by whether you put your faith in Jesus while you were still alive. Jesus identified only two possible locations in the afterlife: heaven or hell. Both last forever.

4. Resurrection. You receive a resurrected body. In eternity, every person will experience bodily resurrection. Jesus taught that some will be resurrected to life, but others will be resurrected to

condemnation. And our new bodies will be immortal—that means they can never again experience death.

5.   Repayment. You receive your reward or your retribution (punishment) for eternity based on what you did on earth.

The outcome of Jesus' evaluation of your works will determine the degree of your reward in heaven or of your suffering in hell. There are two keys to your experience of eternity: first, the key of belief, and second, the key of behavior. Although *where* you spend eternity is based on your belief, *how* you spend eternity is greatly influenced by your behavior while you are on earth. Jesus told His disciples that God had given all powers of judgment to Him and no one else.

Your **future** according to Jesus is full of **wonderful experiences**— if you make certain choices **now**.

6. Eternity. You will live forever in the presence or absence of God, experiencing the consequences of your beliefs and actions on earth.

   Jesus taught that an eternal existence awaits everyone. Those who have rejected Him will experience everlasting punishment, while those who have chosen Him will experience eternal life in God's presence. The eternity that Jesus reveals is not just an existence or state of mind, but a real life in a real place.

So let me ask you, what do you think now about what Jesus said about your future? Are you shocked? Worried? Motivated?

I hear kids say things like, "Wow! I never thought about how much of my life was really going to happen after I leave this earth!" And, "If what Jesus says is true, I need to make some changes in how I live, starting right now."

It's true. Your future, according to Jesus, is full of wonderful experiences—if you make certain choices now. And Jesus doesn't want you to waste another minute believing otherwise.

Which brings us to a connection that many miss. Maybe you've already seen it.

The Dot and the Line

Did you notice that everything that happens to you after you die is decided by just one thing—what you do in your life now?

Sometimes I describe this connection between now and the future as the Law of the Unbreakable Link: *Your choices on earth have direct consequences on your life in eternity.*

When two of my children were young teens, I tried to help them understand this remarkable truth with a picture like this:

The dot is small and exists in one little place. The line begins in one place, then takes off across the page. Imagine that the line extends off the page and goes on and on, without end.

The dot stands for your whole life here on earth. For most of us, that's about seventy years.

The line represents your life after death in eternity. That's forever and ever.

Now, don't miss what this means: Jesus showed us that what happens inside the dot determines everything that happens on the line. It's an unbreakable link! Even a small choice in the dot can result in a huge, long-lasting consequence in eternity.

Does this little illustration help you see your life in a new way?

I remember one dad who was stunned to realize that he had been picturing his life all wrong. He told me, "I can't believe I've prepared for my family vacation and my children's college education and my old age without giving one thought to my *real* future!"

Joseph, a straight-A high school senior and a committed Christian, told me he figured he was

R THE SON OF MAN WILL COME IN THE GLORY OF HIS FATHER

making wise choices about his future—until he thought about the dot and the line. "When I think back over the last few months," he said, "I can't think of any decision I made about my life that had anything to do with eternity."

Can you identify? Would you say you've been living for the line or for the dot?

My friend, you don't need to wonder or worry about what's waiting for you on the other side of your last heartbeat. If you listen closely to what Jesus said, you can know exactly how to change your life so your actions today will count in a positive way for a billion years!

And it can all begin with just one small choice. Just ask a group of dinner guests....

FOR THE SON OF MAN WIL

Let's Talk about It

1. If you could know one thing about the future, what would it be and why?

2. Why do you think so many people in our world are fascinated by Ouija boards, horoscopes, and psychics? What does the Bible say about these kinds of activities?

3. What was the most surprising thing you learned from the timeline—and how is it different from what you believed up to now?

4. Would you say you've been living for the dot of today or for the line of eternity? Explain your answer.

5. How will knowing the truth about your eternal future change what you do today? Do you think it will change the course of the rest of your life? If so, how?

COME IN THE GLORY OF HIS FATHER
IH HIS ANGELS

WHEN YOU GIVE A FEAST
INVITE THE POOR THE MAIMED
THE LAME THE BLIND.
AND YOU WILL BE BLESSED

BECAUSE THEY CANNOT REPAY YOU:
FOR YOU SHALL BE
REPAID AT THE RESURRECTION
OF THE JUST

JESUS IN LUKE 14:13-14

what the bible says
about rewards

Jesus said to do a good deed "and you will be blessed."
You know it's true. And besides, you still remember the
day…

You were feeling good. You were even looking
good. And out of nowhere you got the idea to do
something outrageously, well, *good*. Not just nice,
mind you, but something almost Mother Teresa–like.
So…

- You gave away your favorite CD to a girl that
  you don't even like much.
- You helped cranky Mrs. Dinkleheimer at the
  grocery store, then stuck around visiting with
  her all the way to the cash register.

- You (aka "Mr. Just-Pass-the-Refrigerator") signed up for a youth group weekend of fasting and prayer. Even your parents were worried.
- You, right in front of the beautiful, popular crowd at school, sat down next to the kid *no one* sits next to, and you studied for a test together.

And whatever you did, for the rest of the day, you had *that feeling*. It's a feeling saints must have a lot—of being rewarded by God for just doing the right thing. It's great, isn't it?

My family experienced that feeling one day when we pulled off the highway for lunch and decided to buy a meal for a homeless traveler sitting outside the restaurant. When my daughter, Jennifer, presented him with the biggest cheeseburger on the menu, he beamed at her with a toothless smile, and we made a new friend.

I still remember how I felt as our car pulled back onto the interstate. Completely rewarded. All-over warm and fuzzy. Blessed right out of my socks!

That's what Jesus meant by "blessed," right?

Not quite.

In fact, not even a little bit.

What Jesus Said Next

It happened one evening over dinner. Jesus, along with the town's best and brightest, had been invited to the home of a religious leader (Luke 14:1). As guests were finding their places around the table, Jesus watched them jockey for the best seats.

Suddenly, He spoke up:

> "Sit down in the lowest place.... For whoever exalts himself will be humbled, and he who humbles himself will be exalted."
>
> vv. 10–11

You can almost see everyone squirming in their seats. But Jesus wasn't finished. He turned to the host and told him about a better way to throw a party:

> "When you give a dinner or a supper, do not ask your friends, your brothers, your relatives,

nor rich neighbors, lest they also invite you back, and you be repaid."

v. 12

What an awkward moment! Right in front of everyone, Jesus seemed to be telling the host, "Next time, don't invite all these people you invited tonight." Then Jesus said:

"When you give a feast, invite the poor, the maimed, the lame, the blind. And you will be blessed."

vv. 13–14

Blessed. There's that word again. *And this is where most readers stop!* We remember that blessed feeling we get when we go out of our way to do a good work for someone in need. And we're sure that's all Jesus was talking about.

What kind of paycheck do you think you might have coming?

But look at what Jesus said next:

"And you will be blessed, because they cannot repay you; for you shall be repaid at the
resurrection of the just."

v. 14

Do you see the big idea hiding in Jesus' words?
You will be blessed because "you shall be repaid at
the resurrection"!

I'll bet that not a single guest at that dinner party
missed Jesus' shocking revelation. You will be blessed,
not because of how you feel or don't feel at the time,
but because God will repay you for your good work
after you are dead.

But maybe you noticed something strange here.
Did Jesus actually say "repay," as in giving you back
something real and valuable for something you did?
That doesn't sound anything close to "the free gift of
salvation" you've probably heard about, does it?

So what did Jesus mean?

It's Greek to Me

I remember hearing about a missionary friend in Africa who preached a whole sermon on "The Ten Character Traits of God." He really got into it, and so did the audience. They *loved* his sermon. But afterward, an African friend took him aside and told him that he had used the right word for "character traits" but the wrong sound. Turns out he had preached the first sermon ever on "The Ten Toes of God."

The meanings of words are slippery, aren't they? Especially when they're written in one language and read in another. So now would be a good time to ask what the original New Testament text says when it talks about "reward" or being "repaid" in heaven.

The Bible uses two different words to describe Jesus' rewards.

One, used in Jesus' teachings in Luke 6, is *misthos*. Literally, it means wages: "Rejoice in that day and leap for joy! For indeed your *misthos* [wages] are great in heaven" (Luke 6:23).

Jesus used the same word later when He spoke of earthly wages: "Call the laborers and give them their *misthos* [wages]" (Matthew 20:8).

Everyone who heard Jesus understood exactly what He meant: "When you labor on earth, your employer gives you *misthos*. And when you labor for Me, I pay you wages too."

The second word used for *reward* in heaven appeared in our dinner story in this chapter. Here Jesus used a compound word, *apodidomai. Apo* means *back,* and *didomai* means *to give.* Combined, *apodidomai* means to give back in return or, put simply, repay:

> "You will be blessed…for you shall be *apo-didomai* [given back in return] at the resurrection of the just."
>
> LUKE 14:14

Jesus also used this term in His well-known story about the Good Samaritan, who stopped to help a traveler that had been beaten and robbed by bandits. When the Samaritan took the injured man to a nearby inn for care, he told the innkeeper, "Take care of him; and whatever more you spend, when I come again, I will *apodidomai* [repay] you" (Luke 10:35).

The rewards of Jesus are a very specific kind of payback for something very specific you do for God. And from Scripture it sounds like if you don't do that very specific act, you won't get the reward.

Does that surprise you like it did me?

Okay, so now we know what the rewards of Jesus *do not* mean. They are not an *award* (like you got when you were voted MVP of your basketball team), or a *tip* ("Here's a little something extra"), or a *token of appreciation* (like a plaque for volunteering at the hospital).

Jesus calls His reward *wages,* or *payback*—something you earn resulting from something you do. Jesus says that when you receive His *apodidomai*, you are being paid back in full measure for what you did on His behalf.

So what kind of paycheck do you think you have coming?

Created for Good Works

Have you been doing good works that God will reward?

I've observed that people around the world know instinctively what a good work is: an act you do for someone that meets a need and honors God. (See page 40, "Portrait of a Life God Rewards.")

The truth is that God created *all* of us for good works. In Ephesians chapter 2, Paul wrote:

> We are His workmanship, created in Christ Jesus for good works, which God prepared beforehand that we should walk in them.
>
> v. 10

he box boy at the supermarket could earn **the same or greater reward** than your favorite Christian musician!

In John 15, Jesus said that a life of good works looks like a grapevine loaded down with luscious, beautiful fruit. In my book *Secrets of the Vine,* we saw how much God wants and works for this kind of fruitfulness in every person's life. Jesus told His disciples,

"By this My Father is glorified, that you bear *much fruit*" (v. 8).

Maybe you're one of those people who thinks that God gets serious about rewards only for people on His A-list:

- Sunday school teachers
- Teens who go on mission trips to other countries
- Billy Graham
- Martyrs for Jesus Christ
- Pastors, nuns, and other "professional" religious people
- Maybe a couple of others you forgot.

As you'll see when we get to chapter 5, every follower of Jesus—with no special training, no cosmetic surgery, and no different circumstances at all—has the same opportunity to earn God's "Well done!" and receive His reward. That's because God's rewards are always based on *what we do with what we have*.

That means the box boy at the supermarket who's only been a Christian for six months could earn the same or greater reward than your favorite Christian musician!

And if you think God will repay only people who do grand acts of personal sacrifice and not those who do everyday acts of love, you'll be happy to know that Jesus said, "For whoever gives you a cup of water to drink in My name…will by no means lose his *apodidomai* [repayment]" (Mark 9:41). No deed for God will pass by overlooked or unrewarded. Not even one cup of water given in His name.

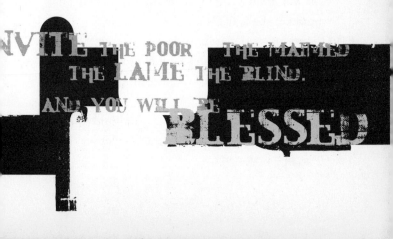

INVITE THE POOR, THE MAIMED, THE LAME, THE BLIND. AND YOU WILL BE BLESSED

Portrait of a Life God Rewards

The teachings of Jesus show many ways we can honor God and earn His reward. Here are what I call the Seven S's of a life God rewards:

1. God will reward you for seeking Him through spiritual acts such as fasting and praying (Matthew 6:6; Hebrews 11:6).
2. God will reward you for submitting to authority as unto Him (Matthew 24:45–47; Ephesians 6:8; Colossians 3:22–24).
3. God will reward you for self-denial in His service (Matthew 16:24–27).
4. God will reward you for serving those in need in His name (Mark 9:41).
5. God will reward you for suffering for His name and reputation (Luke 6:22–23).
6. God will reward you for sacrifices you make for Him (Luke 6:35). In fact, Jesus said that every person who sacrifices to follow Him will be rewarded a hundredfold (Matthew 19:29)!
7. God will reward you for sharing your time, talent, and treasure to further His kingdom (Matthew 6:3–4; 1 Timothy 6:18–19).

The Heart of the Rewarder

I've noticed that people who are making these discoveries for the first time respond with a wide range of feelings. Some experience intense gratitude; some, a burst of anticipation. But others tell me they are reluctant to believe what they're hearing. They'll say, "But I don't deserve any reward!" Or, "If I'm spending eternity with Jesus in heaven, why would I want or need anything more?"

I understand these feelings. I had them myself when I first explored this topic. In fact, I didn't agree with God's plan at all! I'd been happily working for God for years. I couldn't believe that God would want to reward me for what I was already willingly doing for Him. After all, Jesus died for me. Serving Him was the least I could do for Him!

Then one day I reencountered a familiar verse that changed my thinking on this matter once and for all.

ECAUSE THEY CANNOT REPAY YOU;
FOR YOU SHALL BE REPAID

You'll find this verse in Hebrews, nestled in a passage about heroes who pleased God with their faith. "Without faith it is impossible to please Him," the writer says, "for he who comes to God must believe that He is, and that He is a *rewarder*" (11:6).

If you look up that word *rewarder* in the Greek, you'll be amazed by what you discover. The word used here is neither *misthos* nor *apodidomai,* but an unusual combination of both. In fact, Hebrews 11:6 is the only verse in the Bible where you'll find it used to describe a person. God is the *misthos-apodidomai*— the rewarder who pays back your wages in return.

Would God command you to believe that He's a rewarder—then get upset at you if you thought of Him that way? That makes no sense!

You see, God chooses to reward because it is an expression of His own generous nature. His plan to reward, like His provision to save, is a display of His amazing grace.

And there's no other way to think about it. The Bible says that if you want to please God, you must believe that "He is," but you also *must* believe something else: that God is your rewarder.

Today, this takes faith. But in the next chapter, I'll take you to the day in your future when Jesus will prove it to you face-to-face.

Let's Talk about It

1. Can you remember a time when you did something good for someone—and it felt wonderful? What was it?

2. How does knowing that you have a reward coming for that act make you feel? Why do you think this is so?

3. How does knowing about God's plan to reward your works change the way you think about Him?

4. Besides rewards, what are some good and biblical motives for doing good works?

5. Which of the seven *S*'s in the "Portrait of a Life God Rewards" box best describes something you do often? Which of these *S*'s would you like to see in your life more?

ould God COMMAND you to believe that He's a rewarder—
then get UPSET at you if you thought of
Him that way?

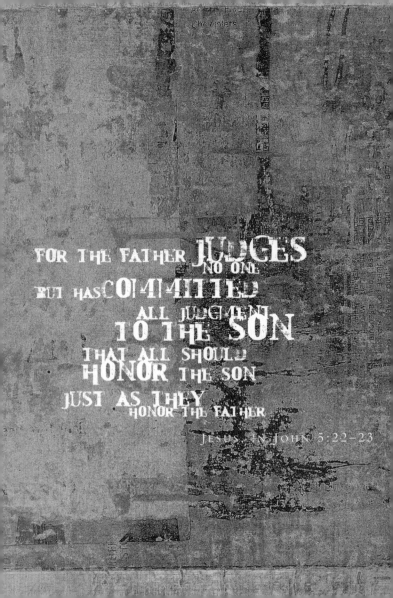

FOR THE FATHER JUDGES NO ONE
BUT HAS COMMITTED
ALL JUDGMENT
TO THE SON
THAT ALL SHOULD
HONOR THE SON
JUST AS THEY
HONOR THE FATHER

JESUS IN JOHN 5:22–23

CHAPTER 4

God's awards ceremony

"My dream is to be in the Olympics and get a gold medal," said Sarah when she was a little girl. "I can't wait for that to happen."

One day it did. Sarah Hughes, by then a high school junior from Great Neck, New York, skated out into the rink at the Winter Olympics. But she was in fourth place, so she decided to forget the pressure and just skate for the pure joy of it.

Did you watch her skate on TV? You would remember if you did. Sarah whirled, she raced, she leaped and swooped. During the entire performance, she grinned from ear to ear. And she made history— she was the first Olympic skater ever to accomplish two perfect triple-triple jumps in the same program.

When the judges' scores rolled in, a deafening roar went up from the crowd. Cameras zoomed in, showing Sarah and her coach on their knees, hugging each other and shrieking. Then Sarah's coach pressed Sarah's face in her hands and said, "You just won the gold medal in the Olympics!"

One day, the grandstands of heaven will thunder and shake with celebration—for you! Why? Because you will have finished the race of your life. Your moment to receive the Judge's reward will have arrived!

The apostle Paul was thinking about his awards ceremony in heaven when he wrote: "There is laid up for me the crown of righteousness, which the Lord, the righteous Judge, will give to me on that Day, and not to me only but also to all who have loved His appearing" (2 Timothy 4:8).

Are you, like Paul, looking forward to God's awards ceremony? Or do you secretly wonder if God would actually give ordinary, sinful old you a reward on your big day in heaven? Either way, this chapter is packed with good news. You're going to find out why Paul could be so sure that his big day in front of the grandstands of heaven would be the very best day of his life…

And why it can be the best day of your life, too.

Paul at the Bema

This chapter takes you to Event 5 on the real timeline of your life: Repayment. We're going to answer important questions like, *How will Jesus evaluate what I did for Him?* And, *What could I win or lose?*

Paul had a lot to say about that day, maybe because of something that happened to him in the Greek city of Corinth. He had been living there for several months, spreading the news of the gospel, when trouble hit. His enemies dragged him into court and accused him of "persuading the people to worship God in ways contrary to the law" (Acts 18:13, NIV).

The exact place where Paul stood before the judge is still visible today in the ruins of Corinth. I've been there several times. You can clearly see the raised marble platform where the judge sat to hear Paul's case. The platform is called the *bema,* which is the Greek word for *judgment seat.* In New Testament times, the very same word was used to describe the stand where judges sat at athletic contests.

It didn't take long for the judge at Paul's hearing to decide that no crime had occurred. Paul was free to go. End of story.

Well, not quite…

Three years later, Paul sent a letter back to the church in Corinth. The bema was on his mind. This time, he talked about a bema in heaven where every follower of Jesus would one day stand:

> For we must all appear before the judgment seat [bema] of Christ, that each one may receive the things done in the body, according to what he has done, whether good or bad.
>
> 2 CORINTHIANS 5:10

Don't miss the shocking and important news in this verse:

Are you ready to imagine the scene on "the

- "All" means *everybody*. All Christians—no exceptions—will be judged.
- The phrases "each one" and "according to what he has done" show that we'll all be judged on an *individual* basis. (You won't get a gold medal for what someone else did, or for what your youth group did if you weren't part of it.)
- "Receive" shows that *we will get something important* that we didn't have before.
- "Things done in the body" means that *we'll receive a reward only for things we did while we were alive on earth*. (That means no more opportunities to change your results.)

Paul is saying exactly what Jesus revealed earlier, isn't he? But he emphasizes an important fact: *The judge you stand before at the end of your life will be none other than Jesus Christ Himself.*

This makes sense. Can you imagine any other person in the universe who could be perfectly fair about your works from heaven's perspective *and* perfectly understanding of your life from your perspective? In fact, Jesus told His disciples He would be their judge when He said: "For the Father judges no one, but has committed all judgment to the Son" (John 5:22).

Are you ready now to imagine the scene on "that Day" with you in it? There you are…

You're in heaven…

You're standing alone before the bema…

Your life on earth is behind you…

Your life in eternity is ahead of you…

You're about to receive your eternal reward…

And the Person looking down at you from the platform, with perfect understanding and great anticipation, is Jesus.

Let me ask you: Do you feel that you are living in such a way right now that you can look forward to that day with great anticipation, or with something less?

Show and Test

Paul gave an even fuller description of that moment in another passage. Instead of describing a platform, he described a building, which was a symbol of all your accomplishments in your life on earth. The foundation is Jesus (1 Corinthians 3:11). But Paul said your building would be tested by fire:

> Now if anyone builds on this foundation with gold, silver, precious stones, wood, hay, straw, each one's work will become clear; for the Day will declare it, because it will be revealed by fire.

vv. 12–13

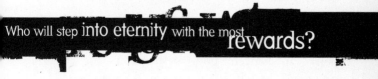

Who will step into eternity with the most rewards?

The first purpose of the bema, then, is to *show* your works. Notice the key words—*become clear, declare,* and *revealed.* At a time of accounting after Jesus comes, all that you have done for God will be plainly and completely revealed.

A second purpose of the bema is to test your works:

> The fire will test each one's work, of what sort it is. If anyone's work which he has built on it endures, he will receive a reward. If anyone's work is burned, he will suffer loss; but he himself will be saved, yet so as through fire.
>
> vv. 13–15

Notice that *your beliefs* aren't being tested (that happened at the moment of your death). *Your sin* isn't being tested (that has already been forgiven and forgotten by God because of what Jesus did for you). And *your destination* in eternity isn't being tested (since you're in heaven, your destination was already decided by your belief in what Jesus did).

So what is tested at the bema?

Your works. What you did with your life for God. Either your works will endure like gold, silver, and precious stones in a fire, or they will burn up like straw. If they burn, not a trace will remain, no matter how enjoyable or even religious those activities might have seemed while you were alive.

Let's say you're waiting off to the side at the bema for your moment before Jesus the Judge. Two people you knew well on earth are ahead of you. One was a student leader in high school who grew up to be a lawyer and a church elder. The other was a shy kid who ended up selling hot dogs from a bicycle cart and cleaning the church as a volunteer. First one and then the other steps forward to receive his reward. Each in turn sees every work he did for God piled high on the altar. Then his pile is tested by fire.

Here's the question: Which of these two will step into eternity with the most rewards?

The answer is that before the fire of the bema, *we can't possibly know*. Until then, only God knows how much of any person's work for Him is rewardable. That's why Paul encouraged Christians to "judge nothing before the time, until the Lord comes.... Then each one's praise will come from God" (1 Corinthians 4:5).

Only after the test by fire will we finally see how a person's life has really added up for eternity. Then the fire will make the truth obvious to all. And when we see it, we will completely agree with the judgment of Jesus and the reward or loss that follows.

Which brings us to ask, what did Paul mean by those two troubling words, "suffer loss"?

"How Could I Lose in Heaven?"

The tested-by-fire passage in 1 Corinthians 3 ends with the words: "If anyone's work is burned, he will *suffer loss;* but he himself will be saved, yet so as through fire" (v. 15).

This is the part about our futures that so few people I know have ever grasped: When we stand before the bema of Jesus, though we cannot lose our salvation, *we may suffer loss.*

What a startling thought! Is it possible that a true follower of Jesus could step into eternity with little or nothing to show for his or her lifetime on earth?

Yes. The apostle John warned, "Look to yourselves, that we do not lose those things we worked for, but that we may receive a full reward" (2 John 1:8). It seems clear from these passages that you could even do a work and then later, because of something you did, miss out on the full reward you had coming.

Here's an example. Let's say a guy at your high school heads up a Bible study for athletes for two years. But then he is caught cheating on his history final and is suspended from school for a week. When the truth comes out, a lot of kids decide that Christians are hypocrites, and many athletes drop out of the Bible study. Will the young man receive his full reward for his good work with the athletes?

You see, our sins will not be revisited at the bema—they are forgiven and forgotten forever because of what Jesus did on the cross. Yet do you see how our sins can still cause us to suffer loss of potential rewards or full rewards at the bema? No wonder

Nothing will compare to the prize of seeing joy and pleasure on Jesus' face as He leans forward to give you and me the reward He most wants to give.

**Three truths about the bema that
can change my life today:**

*Because God is fair, Jesus will judge my works.
So I know that my life matters completely!*

*Because God is generous,
He will reward me for my works.
So I can count on Him to notice and greatly
care about my efforts to please Him!*

*Because God will reward me in heaven,
my eternity will be changed by what I do here.
So what I do for Him today matters eternally!*

John pleaded, "Little children, abide in Him, that when He appears, we may have confidence and not be ashamed before Him at His coming" (1 John 2:28).

Join me in living wholeheartedly for a day of celebration, not disappointment, at the bema. Nothing we could experience on earth will compare to the prize of seeing joy and pleasure on Jesus' face as He leans forward to thank us for the work of our lives, then gives you and me the reward He most wants to give.

A Reward to Keep

Whatever happens at the bema, Jesus will not love you any less or any more for all eternity than He loved you when He purchased your life with His own blood—or than He loves you right now as you're reading this book.

On "that Day," when Jesus gives you the reward for your life—when you finally and completely see and understand all that God has done for you and in you and through you your entire life—your overwhelming response will be to cry out in worship and praise to Him. You'll want to fall at the feet of the Lord Jesus Christ and give back everything He has just given to you.

But let me leave you with one more surprise. Jesus wants you to keep it all.

Why? Because the *misthos* and *apodidomai* of Jesus are not temporary but *eternal* rewards—the lasting consequence of your choice to serve Him during your brief time on earth, and the lasting proof of His love. And because, as I'll show you in the next two chapters, the rewards you receive in heaven will determine a lot about what you actually *do* there.

Let's Talk about It

1. Think about a time when you had to take a very important test. How did you prepare?

2. Why do you think God chooses to test all our works in heaven—at one event?

3. If your works for God were tested by fire today, how much do you think would survive to be rewarded? Explain your answer.

4. How does knowing that one day God will

make everything just and fair for every single person help you cope with all the injustice in the world?

5. Do you look forward to the bema—or do you feel unprepared and anxious? How could either emotion help motivate you today?

FOR THE FATHER JUDGES NO ONE BUT HAS COMMITTED ALL JUDGMENT TO THE SON THAT ALL SHOULD HONOR THE SON JUST AS THEY HONOR THE FATHER

DO
BUSINESS TILL
I COME

JESUS, IN LUKE 19:13

the outrageously enormous business of your life

"How do you make a thousand dollars when all you have in your pocket is a quarter?"

I remember posing the question to my wife, Darlene Marie. We were starting a family and trying to get by on what I earned as a first-year college instructor, which wasn't much. A big night out for us was toasted cheese and Coke on the front porch. Something had to change.

A few days later, I used the quarter to call my father. I had spotted a run-down house for sale that I thought I could fix up for a profit. Would he lend me the down payment? Dad agreed and sent $3,000.

The house was ugly, the paint was peeling, and

the roof leaked. In the back bedrooms, a field of mushrooms had sprouted in the orange shag carpet. I got started cleaning the place up right away, but soon I realized I had another problem—I did not have enough time to remodel and keep up with my teaching.

Then one day I remembered that a builder friend of mine was out of work. I proposed another deal: If he would provide the skilled labor, I would buy the supplies. When we were done, we could split the profit.

He thought it was a great idea. So while I taught, he remodeled. Three months later, I sold the house. After dividing the earnings with my partners, I took home $14,000—more money than my entire year's salary!

My investment of one quarter had yielded a huge return. In business terms, you'd call that leverage—using a little to get back a lot.

This chapter is about investing what God's given you now—your time, your talents, your opportunities—for an *outrageously enormous payoff in eternity.*

Actually, you're going to see that working toward a huge return on the investment of your life is not just a good option; it's what Jesus expects from every single one of us.

Pocket Change

And it always starts with the twenty-five cents you have—*and I'm not even talking about money!*

What do I mean? Well, a quick review of how you're using your time and talents can tell you in very practical terms whether you're living a life today that God will reward. All you have to do is ask yourself this question: *What am I doing with what I have?*

At a youth group meeting not long ago, we went around the circle answering the question "What is my quarter?" Here are some examples of what I heard:

- "People like talking to me. I think it's because I'm a good listener."
- "I'm told I can really sing well, and I love music."

- "I like physical work—anything outdoors."
- "I guess I'm pretty good with details, planning, that kind of thing."
- "Sorry, but my answer is 'Nothing. Nada. Zip!' I'm a big fat zero." (Was Enrique in for a surprise! Within thirty seconds, the other kids helped him see that he was by far the best encourager and motivator in the group.)

Empty your pockets. What unique talent or opportunity do you see in your hands with your name on it?

Your first reaction may be like Enrique's, but God wants to show you that He made you in a particular way and put you in particular circumstances for a very good reason. Starting today, you can invest the time and talents and interests you already have and change your life in eternity.

The Greatest Expectations

Jesus told stories that might sound like bedtime tales, but don't kid yourself. The more you think about what Jesus really said, the more His stories sound like the first explosions of a revolution.

Take the Parable of the Minas, found in Luke 19. Minas were an amount of money, but it's clear from the story that Jesus was talking about a lot more than money in His parable.

When we're talking about living for God, outrageously, enormously, and huge are just other words for ...normal.

In the story, a nobleman must leave town. He calls his servants together, gives each one a mina (about three years' wages), and tells them, "Do business till I come" (v. 13). Then he leaves on a long journey.

When the nobleman returns, he calls the servants together and asks for a report. The first servant has been an exceptional businessman, increasing his master's investment ten times. The master responds, "Well done, good servant; because you were faithful in a very little, have authority over ten cities" (v. 17).

The second servant hasn't done bad either. He reports a fivefold return, and as you'd expect, the nobleman rewards him with authority over five cities. But interestingly, the second servant *doesn't* hear, "Well done," or "good servant," or even "because you were faithful in a very little." Clearly, the master knows he could have done more.

And what about the third servant?

He walks in with the same mina he was given, explaining that he kept the master's money safely hidden at home.

Imagine his shame when the nobleman calls him a "wicked servant" (v. 22) and then takes his one mina and gives it to the servant who already has ten!

Clearly, doing nothing is a very bad option. Even doing pretty well doesn't get a significant enough return. Only taking what you've been given and investing it for an *outrageously, enormously huge return for God's purposes* will result in a full reward.

Because when we're talking about living for God, *outrageously, enormously,* and *huge* are just other words for...*normal.*

You Are What You Believe

Something very powerful caused each of the servants to act in the way they did. In fact, all three servants in Jesus' story made sensible decisions *based on what they believed*. And each one's actions directly impacted his future reward.

But only one of them believed the whole truth…and that made all the difference.

The First Servant's Secret. He knew that the nobleman he worked for expected him to use everything in his power to increase the value of what he'd been given. He knew that once the master returned, all his efforts would be worth it—and more. And what a reward it was—rulership over ten entire cities for simply taking his commission seriously, one mina at a time!

How does this compare to what you believe? A lot of Christians I know think that even though God gave us our gifts and talents, He is not really bothered if we don't make the most of them. *And anyway,* they think, *our works for God won't make any difference in heaven.*

But the truth is that God expects us to take the resources of our lives and *greatly multiply* them for His kingdom. The result? We will have a *great reward!*

The Second Servant's Assumption. He didn't make a terrible mistake, did he? He just wasn't thinking as clearly as he should have been. Maybe he thought that his master's reward would be based on his efforts or his good intentions. He did try. And the master did reward him. But think what could have been!

Does the second servant's attitude remind you of anyone you know? Most Christian teens I meet today think that God counts only effort, not results. Or they think that if God does reward us in heaven for what we do for Him on earth, His reward will be a general "Well done" for everyone.

But the truth is that God cares deeply about results. And He will generously reward our work for Him—in *direct proportion* to how much we have multiplied our life for Him.

The Third Servant's Mistake. What was this servant thinking? That the mina belonged to him and he could do whatever he wanted with it? That his master didn't really mean it when he said, "Do business till I come"? That his master would never return anyway? That he couldn't possibly succeed with just one little mina?

When I teach on this parable, people often rush to defend the third servant. "Wasn't he just being careful?" they say. "Besides, he didn't lose anything."

But think about how you decide who should get more opportunity: You're the captain of the volleyball team. Who do you go to for game point—the player who just shows up every game, or the player who really comes through in a crunch? Parents, teachers, coaches, and employers all work on the same principle—*we give the greatest future opportunity to the person who has done the most with his present opportunity.*

The truth is that doing nothing for God is not okay or even smart. If we don't use for Him what

ho do you go to for game point—
the player who just shows up every game,
or the player who really comes through in a crunch?

God has placed in our care, we will *suffer loss* (remember what Paul said could happen at the bema?). The third servant lost both the potential reward he could have earned and the opportunity to serve his master more fully in the future.

Different Ability, Equal Opportunity

Maybe by now you're thinking, *I don't have many talents or opportunities, so how can I bring God much return for my life? And if that's true, then I don't have the same chance to earn God's reward as a more talented person.*

Jesus brought wonderful and encouraging news for you! But first, let me tell you a family story.

When our son David was in elementary school, he struggled terribly with math. One night he told me, "My best friend doesn't even study, and he gets an A every time. I work three hours a night and I can barely get a C!"

Life just didn't seem fair to him. I sat down with him. "David," I asked, "what percentage of your friend's abilities do you think he is really using in class?"

"Not very much," said David, "maybe half."

I asked, "And what percentage are you using?"

"Almost all of it!"

Then I asked, "Who gave you your strengths, and who gave you your weaknesses?"

"God, I guess," he answered.

"Right," I said. "So He wouldn't expect the same results from one of your weaknesses as He would from one of your strengths, would He?"

David agreed. Then I told him that he should remember that every paper at school gets two grades—one from his teacher and one from God. And God's grades are always based on potential. Just knowing that God didn't expect him to be someone he wasn't helped David enjoy school, and even succeed there—all the way through to a master's degree!

Jesus gave you and me the same encouragement in the Parable of the Talents (Matthew 25:14–30). The story follows the same pattern as the Parable of the Minas. But this time, three stewards are each given *different amounts* of money—"to each according to his own ability" (v. 15).

The third servant in this story makes the same mistake and suffers the same unhappy fate. But the two servants who have doubled what they were given receive equal praise and reward *even though they started—and ended—with different amounts.* Why? Because a servant's reward is based on total results in light of potential—*what each one was capable of doing.*

In the same way, Jesus will reward you and me on the basis of what each of us did with what we were given. Every disciple has the same opportunity to serve God now, and the same opportunity for great reward later.

Never again do you need to envy the person next to you who seems more talented, attractive, or blessed than you! Now you know that in the kingdom of heaven, everyone will be accountable for what they were given, and "to whom much is given, from him much will be required" (Luke 12:48)!

In fact, your future is as promising and important as the future of the most gifted person in history.

Your Ten-Mina Adventure

Are you ready to ask the ten-mina question: *How could I bring God an outrageously, enormously huge return for what He's entrusted me with today?*

If you're not sure where to begin, start by asking yourself what you love doing most. Which of your gifts do you wish were even greater? What is ultimately most fulfilling to you?

For Josh, a high-energy teenager from Virginia, ten-mina living means skiing competitively and speaking to school kids about how to overcome their disabilities. "Everyone has them," he says. "Mine is just more noticeable." You see, Josh lost a leg to cancer when he was nine. (His favorite question came from another high schooler after he had demonstrated how his artificial leg works. She asked, "Is the foot fake too?" "It was a perfect setup," he said. "I told her, 'No, they actually managed to sew my real foot back on.' After she thought about her question, we both laughed until we had tears in our eyes.")

For fourteen teenage girls in Mongolia, ten-mina living meant setting out to change their city for

Christ. That was in 1993. There was no church in their city and probably fewer than one hundred Christians in the whole country. At last count, the church in their city has grown to more than six hundred. "Teenage girls!" wrote one surprised mission director. "The Holy Spirit really has worked in unique ways in Mongolia!"

These two stories are remarkable, but remember, each of us is asked by our Master only to pull all of our potential out of our pocket *and put it to work for Him.*

What ten-mina adventure is God waiting for you to sign up for?

Remember, everything you do for God today is preparing for your (real) forever life in heaven. Serve Him well here, and He'll reward you with more opportunity to serve Him well in eternity.

I guarantee that the best adventures and most amazing results come when we start with the one mina we have…and decide to settle for nothing less than bringing back ten more for God.

Let's Talk about It

1. How would you describe your own "quarter" in terms of your unique talents or opportunities?

2. Up to now, have you been actively investing and growing what God has given you, or have you assumed it didn't matter that much to Him? Explain your answer.

3. How do you feel about the fact that you are preparing on earth for what you will do in heaven? For you, is this great news, nerve-racking news, or something in-between?

4. Does the news that God evaluates your work based on your own unique personal potential make you think you're doing better than you thought or worse? Why?

5. What could you do this week to turn your one mina into ten for God's kingdom?

DO NOT LAY UP FOR YOURSELVES

TREASURES ON EARTH
WHERE MOTH
AND RUST DESTROY

AND WHERE

THIEVES BREAK IN AND STEAL;

BUT LAY

UP FOR YOURSELVES
TREASURES
IN HEAVEN

WHERE NEITHER MOTH NOR
RUST DESTROYS AND WHERE THIEVES
DO NOT BREAK IN AND STEAL.

JESUS, IN MATTHEW 6:19–20

the treasure movers

For three thousand years, the king's body lay in total darkness, deep inside a mountain in the Egyptian desert…until 1922, when an archaeologist named Howard Carter found the tunnel that led to the door of the tomb and cracked the tomb open.

"At first I could see nothing," Carter later said. "The hot air escaping from the chamber caused the candles to flicker. But as my eyes grew accustomed to the light, details emerged from the mist—strange animals, statues, and gold…everywhere the glint of gold."

Carter had discovered the burial treasures of King Tutankhamen, a pharaoh who died while he was still a teenager. Tut's tomb was filled with almost unimaginable treasure—golden chariots, a fleet of miniature ships, the king's golden throne, statues of slaves, childhood toys, jewelry, food, and more. And the mummy itself rested inside a solid gold coffin.

Did you ever wonder why a pharaoh would hide so much treasure in a hole in the ground? I mean, what could it do for him *after he was dead?*

The answer is that the ancient Egyptians took the afterlife very seriously. They believed that this life was a preparation for the next life, and the next life was the best one, so the more possessions you could take from earth, the better. In fact, just before temple priests sealed King Tut's tomb, they pried open his mouth so he would be able to eat and drink on the journey to his new life. (Now you know why Egyptian mummies always look like they're laughing—or is it screaming?)

Actually, King Tut had it right…almost. You see, treasure will matter in heaven, and it will matter *a lot!* But in Tut's case, "almost right" turned out to be dead wrong. His gold never made it out of that hole in the desert.

BUT LAY UP FOR YOURSELVES TREASURES

My friend, Jesus came to show us a better way. In the previous chapter we looked at what Jesus said about investing our *time* and *talents* for Him. His amazing revelation was that if we use what He's loaned us on earth for His purposes—and use it to greatly multiply His kingdom—He will greatly reward us in heaven.

In this chapter we look at a third *t*-word—*treasure*. You're going to discover that you were born to succeed where King Tut failed. The treasure of your life is meant to add up to a fortune, something that will shine for all eternity…something more valuable even than gold.

The Treasure of Your Life

What is treasure? And do you have any?

Technically, treasure is your money and your possessions. It's extremely valuable and worth working for. Treasure is something you can hold and want to carefully guard, and would be extremely sorry to lose.

And yes, you have some! You might be thinking, *I can skip this chapter since I don't have any gold*. But try this: Make a list of every possession you can think of that you would hate to lose if, say, you were robbed or your house burned to the ground. Your treasure might be your clothes, your favorite CDs, your money, or your car. One girl's list had twenty-nine things on it—twenty-two music posters, six dolls, and one pet iguana.

Listen, some of the most materialistic people I've ever met are teenagers who have hardly any money! And I've met them all around the world. How can I say such a thing? Because these young people think about treasure all the time. They make all their decisions in order to get more money or possessions (or to guard what they have), and they judge other people based almost entirely on what they own and how much it cost.

Does what I'm saying remind you of kids you know? Does it remind you of yourself? If so, listen carefully to what Jesus had to say on this subject. You're going to be pleasantly surprised, and maybe even shocked.

Storing your **treasure** in heaven isn't selfish either—it's God's will

"Lay Up for Yourselves…"

Perhaps Jesus' most familiar teaching on treasure is found in the Sermon on the Mount:

> "Do not lay up for yourselves treasures on earth, where moth and rust destroy and where thieves break in and steal; but lay up for yourselves treasures in heaven."
>
> MATTHEW 6:19–20

If you grew up in church like I did, you may have the wrong idea about what this verse is saying. I always thought Jesus was pointing out that spiritual treasures are more important than earthly ones.

But that's not it at all!

Jesus used the same word to describe treasure on earth as He did to describe treasure in heaven. Why? So you would know that treasure in heaven is still…treasure.

Treasure in heaven is completely real and eternally valuable.

So real and valuable, in fact, that Jesus once told a very wealthy man that if he wanted to own treasure in heaven too, he should sell *everything* he owned on earth (Matthew 19:21)!

I find three truths in the verses above that nearly everyone misses:

1. *Jesus said you should "lay up" treasure in heaven.* To lay up means to stockpile or accumulate on purpose. And the Greek verb, translated "lay up" is not a suggestion, but a command! Jesus is saying, "Do it! It's God's will for you."

2. *Jesus said you should lay it up "for yourselves."* No one else can do it for you. Storing your treasure in heaven isn't selfish either—it's God's will, and it's the only way. No wonder Jesus called a man who didn't store up treasure in heaven a fool (Luke 12:13–21).

3. *Jesus said lay it up "in heaven."* Jesus never said owning treasure is wrong. He only wanted you to know that treasure on earth isn't safe. Only in heaven does treasure have lasting value to you.

This brings us back to King Tut's trouble with treasure—how do you actually move your treasure from earth to heaven?

God's Moving Plan

Tut's moving plan was to hoard as much as possible, then keep it close by after death so it could be used when it was needed. But mummies don't have a lot of personal needs, not even for gold.

God's plan is pretty much the opposite: *To move your treasure to heaven, you have to let it go and send it on ahead.*

How do we accomplish that? Jesus explained His moving plan to His disciples:

> "Sell what you have and give alms; provide yourselves money bags which do not grow old, a treasure in the heavens that does not fail, where no thief approaches nor moth destroys."

> LUKE 12:33

This verse clearly shows that there is a link between what you do with your treasure on earth and what happens as a result in heaven. If you "give alms" (donations and gifts) now, Jesus told His friends, you will actually "provide [for] yourselves" something incredibly valuable later—"a treasure in the heavens."

Maybe you always thought that one of God's main goals was to separate you from your treasure. *Why else would those preachers always be asking for offerings?* you wonder.

But I hope that now you see it's just the opposite! Jesus wants you to "provide" for yourself *because* He knows that treasure will matter in eternity, and He wants you to have a lot of it there. And that preacher may be doing you a huge favor by reminding you of how to make God's savings plan work. And believe me, living according to that plan will radically change how you think and act.

Seven young men **shaved off** all their hair to show support a **dying friend** who had lost his hair because of cancer treatments.

Baseball Cards and Shaved Heads

You can probably look around your circle of friends and find your own favorite examples of giving away earthly treasure. Here are a few of mine:

- James sold his old baseball card collection and gave the money to his brother so he could go on a missions trip with his junior high youth group.
- Kirsten donates her car for a day every week to an elderly neighbor who needs to run errands but doesn't have any transportation.
- Seven young men shaved off all their hair to show support for a dying friend who had lost his hair because of cancer treatments.
- Anita gave away four of her favorite sweaters to a financially disadvantaged foreign exchange student who was visiting her family's home.

As you can see, giving is always a very personal choice. But the sooner you start using your treasure for God's work, the more you'll discover how much fun life can be—and how good your God can be.

I suggest you begin by asking two questions:

1. *What treasure has God given me?* Just as with your
   time and talents, God measures faithfulness by
   how much you give of what you have.
   Remember the story from Luke of the widow
   who put only two small coins in the offering?
   Jesus said that, compared to the rich people
   making a show of their big gifts, "this poor
   widow has put in more" (Luke 21:3). You can
   do the work of God on earth starting now, with
   what you already have in your possession.

2. *What is God asking me to do with it?* Give generously to your church; then ask God to show you
   clearly how He wants you to serve Him with
   your money. Not a single possession under your
   control got there by accident. Remember the
   boy who loaned Jesus his lunch by the lake one
   day? Jesus used it to feed thousands—and there
   was food left over (Matthew 14:13–21)! (Did
   you ever wonder how many of the leftover bas-
   kets of food Jesus sent home with the little boy

so he could show his mom what one lunch for God could accomplish?) Jesus can do the same with your prized possessions, no matter how insignificant they might seem at first glance.

But you have to give them to Him first. And as you give them back to Him—first cautiously, then hopefully, then with great anticipation—you'll discover you can never out-give God!

Do you believe me? Will discovered it firsthand one day. I know, because I was there.

A Boy and a Radio

I was taking a coffee break during a family conference in Kentucky when Will walked up and stood beside my chair. He was about nine. He asked if I wanted to donate to a missions project.

"What would you use my money for?" I asked.

Will held out a radio. "This radio runs by sun power," he said proudly. "It's for people who live in the jungles. People can listen to this radio to learn things and hear about Jesus."

I decided on the spot to make Will an offer. "Tell you what," I said, "I'll give to your project, but I have a rule that says you have to give money first." On one of his donation cards, I wrote out my proposal:

Will,
If you give one to five dollars,
    I'll give double what you give.
If you give six to ten dollars,
    I'll give triple what you give.
If you give eleven to twenty dollars,
    I'll give four times what you give.

I signed my name and Will read the card. By the time he was finished, his eyes were as big as saucers. Then suddenly his face fell, and he stared at the floor.

"Don't you like my idea?" I asked.

"Yeah," he said, shuffling his feet.

"Well, what are you going to do?"

"Nothing."

"Nothing?"

"I can't," he said. "I already gave everything I had."

I felt a pang in my heart. "You mean you put all your money in your own fund drive?" I asked.

He nodded.

"So you can't buy any more snacks for the rest of the conference?"

He nodded again.

At that moment, I knew what I needed to do. "Actually, Will," I began, "I also have a rule that if you give everything you have, I will give everything I have, too."

The treasure God asks you to serve Him with can easily become a rival God.

As it happened, I'd just been to a bank to withdraw a considerable amount of cash for my trip. I reached under the table for my briefcase, pulled out a bank envelope of bills, and handed it to Will.

Have you ever done something outrageous, but you just knew was right...and you did it without thinking? That's what happened to me that day. In fact, I'm not sure who was more surprised when I handed over all my money—Will or me! But both of us were grinning happily.

Friend, I want you to know that God's plan to give you treasure in heaven for giving to His work on earth makes my matching plan look like free pennies. God's generosity always outmatches ours!

One day after hearing Jesus talk about treasure in heaven, Peter asked Jesus, "See, we have left all and followed You. Therefore what shall we have?" (Matthew 19:27). Jesus didn't scold Peter for asking, or smile and say, "I wasn't actually serious about treasure in heaven." Instead, He told Peter that he and the other disciples would rule over the nation of Israel when He set up His kingdom. Then He said that every person who has left all to follow Him would inherit eternal life and be repaid a hundredfold (v. 29).

An investment specialist told me once that a hundredfold repayment adds up to a 10,000 percent return!

So why, when we understand how generously God will respond to our giving, would we not serve Him with our treasure?

It's probably because we serve another master *and don't even know it.*

Where Your Heart Is...

You see, the treasure God asks you to serve Him with can easily become a rival god. Jesus said:

> "No servant can serve two masters; for either he will hate the one and love the other, or else he will be loyal to the one and despise the other. You cannot serve God and mammon."
>
> LUKE 16:13

Mammon is another word for money. When you serve God, you are using God's money to accomplish His wishes. But when you serve money, you are using God's money to accomplish your wishes. If you do that, you're not living to please God. You're not living for eternal reward. And you will always want to keep your money here.

But Jesus said, "Where your treasure is, there your heart will be also" (Matthew 6:21).

So let me ask you, where is your heart right now? If you aren't purposefully and generously investing your treasure in what will hold its value in heaven, I promise you it's because your heart isn't there.

The solution is simple, probably difficult, and absolutely life changing—move your heart!

Don't wait for your heart to move on its own, my friend, because it might never happen. Instead, apply what you've learned from the words of Jesus. Begin today to move your treasure to what matters in heaven...and your heart will follow.

Let's Talk about It

1. What would you say are your three most valuable treasures in monetary terms? What about in terms of your heart?

2. On a scale of one to ten, how generous would you say you've been with your possessions up to now (one being "stingy" and ten being "generous")? How might the news of this chapter change your answer in the future?

3. Think of someone you know who appears to be accumulating a lot of treasure on earth. What would you say to them?

4. Why might it take a great deal of faith in order to store up treasure in heaven?

5. What can you do today, right now, to add to your account in heaven?

BUT LAY UP FOR YOURSELVES TREASURES IN HEAVEN WHERE NEITHER MOTH NOR RUST DESTROYS AND WHERE THIEVES DO NOT BREAK IN AND STEAL.

FOR GOD DID NOT SEND HIS SON INTO THE WORLD TO CONDEMN THE WORLD BUT THAT THE WORLD THROUGH HIM MIGHT BE SAVED

JESUS, IN JOHN 3:17

the first
key

Rudy had that look. His wife had just introduced him to me at the front of the church, then "unexpectedly" left to attend to other matters. Rudy stood there awkwardly, hands shoved in his pockets. I'm sure he would have given his life savings to be somewhere else.

I smiled and asked how I could help.

"My wife wants me to get religion," he said, scuffing the carpet with the toe of his shoe. I asked him why.

He frowned. "So I don't go to hell."

"Are you planning to go to hell sometime soon?" I asked.

He looked at me, then burst out laughing. I think

he was relieved to find that a Bible teacher might have a sense of humor.

"So," I continued, "when you stand before God, what's going to keep you out of hell?"

Dead silence. Then Rudy chuckled. "I guess I never thought about it quite like that," he said. "I'm not a bad person, you know. I don't run around on my wife. And I try to be a nice guy...."

I decided to help him out. "So God probably has a big scale, wouldn't you think? On one side would be your sins. You do sin, don't you, Rudy?"

He nodded.

I continued. "And on the other would be all those good things you do for your wife, your kids, your community, and so on. Am I on the right track?"

Rudy nodded with more enthusiasm.

"And when God puts your life on His big scale, you'll have more good than bad, and everything will be okay, right?"

A smile crossed Rudy's face. He liked how my answer was shaping up. I told him that it all made sense to me too. But I had a question.

I took out my pen and drew a line like this on a notepad:

TOTALLY EVIL ————————————— TOTALLY GOOD
(0 percent good)   *(100 percent good)*

I pointed at the line. "So if this line is like a see-saw," I said, "you just need to decide how much more good than bad you need to do in order to tilt the see-saw in your favor." I handed Rudy my pen and asked him to put an *x* on the line to mark how close to "Totally Good" he'd have to get to be good enough for heaven.

Rudy studied the line, then started to mark an *x* at about 60 percent. Then he thought some more and moved the tip of the pen closer to 75 percent. Then he paused to think again. Finally he shook his head and drew a rather feeble *x* at about the 70 percent spot.

He handed back my pen without looking up.

I pointed to his mark. "Let's say you hit your spot right on the nose, Rudy, because you really aren't that bad of a guy. But what if when you meet your Maker, He tells you that, unfortunately, the x spot is farther to the right—say, at 71 percent? If you were 70 percent 'good' but God said the minimum requirement was actually 71 percent, where would a person like you go?"

He crossed his arms. "Hell, I guess."

"Then finding out where the actual x is on that line would be the most important question of your life, right?" I asked.

Rudy grunted. "Yeah," he said. "I'm not sure where it ought to be."

I closed my notepad and started picking up my things, but Rudy wasn't moving. "Are you saying I can know exactly where the x is?" he asked. "Cause I really need to know. Maybe you could show me?"

I was hoping he would feel that way. We found a seat in a quiet corner, and I showed him what the Bible says about that x. He listened carefully and he responded. And in the next few minutes, my new friend hit God's mark perfectly.

Everyone who thinks this way is trying to solve the right problem with the wrong key

"But I'm a Good Person!"

The first six chapters of the book focused on the second key to your eternity, which is your *behavior*. Your behavior—meaning what you do for God while you're alive—decides your reward after you die. So your behavior affects *how* you will spend eternity.

But as you may recall, the first key is *belief*. Your belief decides where you will spend eternity.

Notice that it never entered Rudy's mind that everything was okay between him and God—because he knew it wasn't. He knew he had a problem. That's why where he would spend eternity was still a big question mark to him.

The name for Rudy's problem is *sin*. Rudy knew he had sinned many times. You know you sin too, and all of your friends know they sin.

The Bible says that God put this awareness of our own sin problem inside us:

> But God shows his anger from heaven against all sinful, evil men who push away the truth from them. For the truth about God

is known to them instinctively; God has put this knowledge in their hearts.

ROMANS 1:18–19, TLB

The Bible says that besides knowing about our own sin, we are created to know about God. We know He exists, we know He is righteous (meaning perfectly good and without sin), and we know He wants us to be righteous too. Knowing these two basic facts—our sinfulness and God's righteousness—leaves us without excuse.

Here's how the Bible describes our situation:

Since earliest times men have seen the earth and sky and all God made, and have known of his existence and great eternal power. So they will have no excuse [when they stand before God at Judgment Day]. Yes, they knew about him all right, but they wouldn't admit it or worship him or even thank him for all his daily care.

VV. 20–21, TLB

Everyone knows we deserve God's judgment, so we're desperate to find out what we can do to make things right with Him and escape the consequences of our sin.

Millions of people around the world try, like Rudy did, to fix their sin problem by doing more good works. But everyone who thinks this way is trying to solve the right problem with the wrong key.

Hell is a place you don't want to go, and a place God doesn't want anyone to go.

Here's what I mean:

Jesus taught that our works for God on earth can greatly benefit us in eternity, but only *after* our sin problem has been resolved and heaven is our destination. And Jesus said that the only way to get into heaven is to believe the right thing.

Heaven is not God's reward for doing but His free gift for believing.

But Jesus also wants you to know that if you believe the wrong thing, you'll end up in the wrong eternal destination. It's called *hell*. Hell is a place you don't want to go, and a place God doesn't want *anyone* to go.

Here's a simple question to find out if you're still with me: *To help Rudy solve his problem, did I talk to him about the importance of doing more good works so he could earn more eternal reward? Or did I talk to him about the importance of believing in Jesus so he could receive God's free gift?*

If you chose the second answer—"the importance of believing in Jesus"—you're tracking right with me.

Both our works and our belief are important to God. And both prove His amazing love and generosity to us. But only your belief in Jesus can unlock a future in heaven with Him…and keep you out of hell.

Before I tell you what I told Rudy about avoiding hell, let's take a look behind the curtains of eternity. Jesus wants to show you something…

Hell Is No Party

You've probably heard it. Timothy McVeigh said it before he was executed for killing 168 innocent people with a bomb—"Hell won't be so bad. At least I'll be with all my friends!"

Will hell be one big party? Will it be miserable but temporary—say, until God stops being mad at you, or you have paid enough for your sins?

Jesus wanted all His followers to know the truth about hell. One day Jesus told a story about what it was like there. His story followed two people to their eternal destination (Luke 16:19–23).

The first was a rich man who enjoyed the best of everything.

The other was a beggar named Lazarus who lived off the crumbs that fell from the rich man's table. Lazarus was so weak and wretched that he couldn't even keep the dogs from licking his sores.

But when the two men died, things changed…radically! The beggar went to eternal comfort in heaven—in Jesus' story called "Abraham's bosom." The rich man went to eternal misery in hell.

And that's when the real drama begins. You see, in Jesus' story, the rich man isn't just miserable alone. He can see all the way to heaven. And he can see that there Lazarus is being comforted in the presence of Abraham.

Now it is the rich man's turn to beg. In the conversation that follows (vv. 24–31), Jesus reveals what hell will really be like. I'll paraphrase a little:

Rich man: "Father Abraham, have mercy on me! Send Lazarus with a drop of water to cool my tongue, for I am tormented in this flame!"

Abraham: "Son, between you and us there is a great gulf fixed."

Rich man: "Then I beg you to send Lazarus to earth to talk to my five brothers. Otherwise, they'll end up in this place of torment too!"

Abraham: "They already have the Scriptures. Let them hear the truth there."

Rich man: "Yes, but if someone goes from the dead to talk to my brothers, I know they'll repent!"

Abraham: "If they won't believe what the Bible says, neither will they be persuaded by a witness from the dead."

And that's the end of Jesus' story. The curtains close on heaven and hell...

Jesus' story of the rich man and Lazarus reveals

that hell is no party—and no joke. In this conversation from the afterlife, we learn:

- Hell is a place of torment. People there are conscious; they can communicate; they feel pain and regret—and it will never stop.
- Hell is a place with no exit. Once you enter, you can never leave. There will always be a "great gulf fixed" between you and what could have been.
- Hell is a place that if you knew what it was really like, you would be desperate to let people you love know the truth!

If you already know your destination is heaven, the truth about hell will strongly motivate you to be the one to tell your family and friends how to choose eternal life with God instead of eternal torment without Him.

If you're like Rudy, and you're not sure where you'll spend eternity, isn't it time for you to pick up the key that will unlock heaven for you, personally and forever?

Hell by Degrees

Do you think hell will be the same for everyone? Since Jesus reveals that there will be degrees of reward in heaven, wouldn't it make sense that a just God would judge nonbelievers in the same way—with degrees of punishment?

That's exactly what Jesus said. Specifically, He revealed that suffering in hell has the potential to increase according to how a person lived his life: "And you, Capernaum.... I say to you that it shall be more tolerable for the land of Sodom in the day of judgment than for you" (Matthew 11:23–24). Notice the phrase "more tolerable." The word more indicates that different degrees of tolerability and judgment exist in hell.

On another occasion, Jesus told the Pharisees that they would "receive greater condemnation" for misusing their position (Matthew 23:14). The apostle Paul wrote that some were "treasuring up for [themselves] wrath in the day of wrath" (Romans 2:5).

Here's a helpful way to remember the truth: Heaven never gets worse, only better; hell never gets better, only worse.

Why Works Won't Work

Rudy was ready to learn where the x should go. I pointed to the 100 percent good mark and said, "The Bible says that's where the x has to be."

"But that's impossible!" Rudy said, looking alarmed. "If you have to be perfect, no one can go to heaven."

"So you agree that no one can be 100 percent good and solve the problem of sin on his own?"

"Yes, I guess so," he said.

"What if I told you that the penalty for even one sin is death?"

"Well, that wouldn't seem fair at all," he said. "Everyone sins. Does the Bible really say that even one sin brings the death penalty?"

I opened my Bible and showed Rudy that ever since Adam and Eve sinned in the Garden, death has been the consequence. I asked Rudy to read aloud Genesis 2:17: "For in the day that you eat of it you shall surely die." Then we turned to Romans 6:23 and he saw the sin problem described in the same way in the New Testament: "For the wages of sin is death."

Rudy and I tried to brainstorm a solution. "Let's say I went before a judge and was sentenced to die," I said. "But what if I told the judge, 'Please, sir, let me live, and I promise I'll do a lot of community service'? Would that pay off my death penalty?"

"Not a chance," said Rudy. After a minute he said, "So there's no solution, is there? There's no hope."

"Exactly," I said. "There's no hope—" I paused for a moment before continuing—"unless you could find a substitute. What if someone volunteered to die for you in your place when it came time for God to judge you?"

"That would be great," he said. "But you said they'd have to be 100 percent good, and no one is, right?"

"No one except Jesus," I answered. Then I showed Rudy from the Bible that Jesus is God's Son and that He alone lived on this earth without sin. I showed him that God sent His Son to earth so that He could be Rudy's substitute, die in Rudy's place, and pay the penalty for his sin—and the whole world's sin—once and for all.

Then I pulled out my notebook again. I pointed to the *x* Rudy had drawn. "You have a choice to make, Rudy."

"Okay," he said.

"You can believe in your good works and hope you're right about the *x*. Or you can believe in Jesus Christ and receive the benefit of His death on your behalf."

"Definitely the second choice," he said. "It makes way more sense."

We read together some of my favorite verses:

"For God so loved the world that He gave His only begotten Son, that whoever believes in Him should not perish but have everlasting life. For God did not send His Son into the world to condemn the world, but that the world through Him might be saved."

JOHN 3:16–17

And that's when Rudy made a personal decision that changed his eternal destination for good.

Is there a desire in your heart right now to make the same choice? If you have been reading this chapter and you're not sure that heaven is your destination, I urge you to put your faith in what Jesus said. I invite you right now to pray the same prayer Rudy did:

Dear God, I am sorry for my sins, and now I know I can't do anything to fix them. So I accept Your Son's death as full payment for my sins, and I receive the Lord Jesus Christ as my Savior. And Jesus, I'm going to start serving You right now! In Your name, amen.

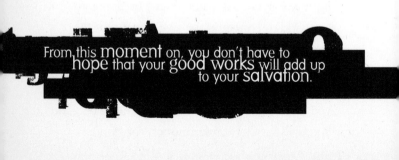

From this moment on, you don't have to hope that your good works will add up to your salvation.

Heaven Bound

If you just put your full trust in Jesus for your salvation, your eternal destination has already permanently changed—from hell to heaven!

Now you are a new creation in Jesus (2 Corinthians 5:17). Now you have eternal life (John 3:16–17). Now you are a child of God with an amazing future (Galatians 4:7).

From this moment on, you don't have to hope that your good works will add up to your salvation, because like every other true follower of Jesus, you now understand the meaning of these well-known verses:

> By grace you have been saved through faith, and that not of yourselves; it is the gift of God, not of works, lest anyone should boast.
>
> EPHESIANS 2:8–9

Because of what Jesus did on the cross for you, and because you have put your faith in Him, you will never experience in eternity the penalty of your sin. Why? Because Jesus paid the penalty for you.

Instead, you can begin responding to God with your whole heart, because you have an important destiny, starting now.

Look at the very next verse:

For we are His workmanship, created in Christ Jesus for good works, which God prepared beforehand that we should walk in them.

v. 10

You see, you and I have been created and saved to do good works! And if you just placed your trust in Jesus Christ, then for the first time in your life, you are truly ready to live a life God rewards.

Let's Talk about It

1. Why is it so important to know that good works don't help you get into heaven? Can you relate to Rudy's confusion?

2. How does it make you feel to know that Jesus paid the penalty of death for sin on your behalf? Do you think that sometimes you take your salvation for granted?

3. Why would staying in a daily and close relationship with Jesus help you do more good works for Him?

4. Do you have any friends who don't understand how to solve the problem of sin? How does knowing the truth about heaven *and* hell change the way you think about talking to them?

5. How could what you learned in this chapter help you explain to your unsaved friends what Jesus did for them?

FOR GOD DID NOT SEND HIS SON INTO THE WORLD TO CONDEMN THE WORLD BUT THAT THE WORLD THROUGH HIM MIGHT BE SAVED

AND **BEHOLD** I AM
COMING QUICKLY AND
MY REWARD IS
WITH ME TO **GIVE**
TO **EVERY ONE**
ACCORDING TO HIS WORK

JESUS, IN REVELATION 22:12

seeing through to forever

When your alarm clock goes off tomorrow morning, eternity will be nowhere in sight.

You'll roll out of bed, head for the bathroom, reach for your toothbrush, look at that face in the mirror…and make the first choice of your new life.

Will I live for what I can see, knowing it will soon disappear?

Or will I live for eternity?

What you can see may be temporary, but it sure is convincing, isn't it? The latest fashion trend. The pop music star you see on every magazine cover. The temptations that pour from your TV or walk by on the street.

But Jesus calls you to live by faith, not by sight.

You see, your faith in what you can't see decides what you will do with your day or your life. It even decides where you call your home....

I'll never forget hearing the story of a missionary couple from Great Britain who had spent their lives serving God in a forgotten corner of the earth. It was the 1800s. Travel was slow and difficult, so the couple didn't return for visits. Years passed. Wars came and went. Finally, the missionaries wrote their supporters to tell them they were coming home. A few months later, the elderly couple sailed for England.

When they laid eyes on their country's coastline for the first time in decades, the man said to his wife, "I wonder if anyone will be here to welcome us home."

As the ship sailed into the harbor, the couple stood at the upper deck of the ocean liner, holding hands. Then, to their surprise, they saw a huge crowd of people on the dock, pointing in their direction and cheering. A band played. Somebody was holding up a banner that read, "Welcome home! We're proud of you!"

The husband was deeply moved. "Isn't this wonderful?" he exclaimed. His wife laughed happily. Then they decided it was time to go below to collect their luggage.

But as they stepped excitedly onto the gangplank that led to the dock, they were taken aback. The crowd had already started to scatter. Soon it became clear what had happened. The huge welcome was not for them, but for a popular politician returning from a foreign success. In fact, no one was there to greet the missionaries at all.

The husband stopped and gave a big sigh. "After a lifetime of service, this isn't much of a welcome home," he said.

His wife took his arm. "Come along, sweetheart," she said softly. "This is just England. We're not home yet."

Do you think of **heaven** as your final destination and your **real** home—or just some **fluffy dream** in the far-off yonder?

At Home in Heaven

Think of heaven as the chosen site for God's family reunion. What are some of the wonders that Scripture tells us about our homecoming?

1. We will all feel God's welcome. Jesus said, "I go to prepare a place for you…that where I am, there you may be also" (John 14:2–3). Heaven will feel like coming home to every child of God. We will all sense God's anticipation and pleasure in our company. Like a good father, He will express delight at our arrival (even if we arrive with muddy shoes or skinned knees).

2. We will all be changed and know that we are changed. When we see Jesus face-to-face, we shall be like Him. In the beginning, God made man in His image—then came sin. When the curse of sin is removed, we will once again reflect the pure and holy image of our Father (Genesis 1:26; 1 John 3:2).

3. We will all worship. Worship will be our natural, unstoppable response to the direct experience of God and His goodness—no choir practice required. In heaven, as we breathe in the fullness of God, we will breathe out thankfulness and praise (Revelation 15:3–4).

4. We will all experience the end of suffering. There'll be no more pain, sorrow, hunger, thirst, loneliness, want, sin, death—no more suffering of any kind. Think of that "no more" not as a loss, but as an ocean-sized promise. Then God will fill that ocean, as He said He would, with His love and goodness.

5. We will all experience a new life in a new world. "Behold, I make all things new," Jesus said (Revelation 21:5). In heaven, God will make every wrong right. Our old life will be over. We will be at rest at last in our new, forever home (Revelation 21:2–5).

Home on the Horizon

This book has tried to show you what Jesus wanted you to know, so that even when your true home is nowhere in sight, you'll still make the right choice! "We do not look at the things which are seen," wrote Paul, "but at the things which are not seen. For the things which are seen are temporary" (2 Corinthians 4:18).

When Jesus was preparing to leave His disciples, He talked about that place. Listen to His words:

> "In My Father's house are many mansions; if it were not so, I would have told you. I go to prepare a place for you. And if I go and prepare a place for you, I will come again and receive you to Myself; that where I am, there you may be also."
>
> JOHN 14:2–3

Think of all the ways Jesus could have described heaven. He could have talked about the streets of gold, the legions of angels, the thrones of the apostles.

But Jesus wanted His followers to know that heaven was first and foremost…*home*.

Let me ask you: Do you think of heaven as your final destination and your real home—or just some fluffy dream in the far-off yonder?

I promise that when you realize that Planet Earth is just stage one of your whole, eternal life, the shape of your days will change radically.

I remember when my wife and I first chose to believe in God's eternal reward and to live for home instead of here. Our priorities changed. How we handled our money, our time, and our abilities changed. We began to see strangers as people Jesus died for so they could be with Him, *at home.*

And every day, we became more grateful, more overwhelmed by the kindness of God.

Since then, we've met hundreds of other people, young and old, who are on an outrageous mission— to live for eternity, starting today.

What are these people like, you ask? They are wealthy businessmen who actually believe they "own" nothing, not even their shoes. They are students who see an adventure for God in every new face, every difficult class, every belittling job. They are young moms who know that their most important work for all of eternity might be the little ones sleeping in the next room.

These pilgrims seem a lot like other people on the surface, but they understand a day's possibilities from a completely different point of view. They see the extraordinary business of eternity lurking in the ordinary business of every day.

Sure, they are living *in* the dot, but they are living *for* the line. They're making a difference for God on the streets of New Delhi and Manchester and Lagos and Biloxi....

But they are already citizens of heaven.

Change of Address

Friend, I believe that God is asking you to make a life-changing decision before you leave this book. You need to change your citizenship from earth to heaven.

The apostle Paul, though he was proud to be both a Jew and a Roman citizen, purposefully chose to think of himself as a citizen of heaven, not of earth (Philippians 3:20). It was a deep longing to be in heaven with his Lord that occupied his thoughts, shaped his values, and ordered the use of his time. The consequence of Paul's choice continues to impact the world for God today.

If you have heard and understood what Jesus revealed about a life God rewards, and if you're ready to make today count for eternity, I encourage you to join me in declaring your new citizenship:

> *Lord Jesus, I have listened carefully to what You said about my home. I believe You, and I can't wait to be there with You. Thank You for the gift of my life on this earth, but from this day on, I will live as a citizen of heaven—my true home. I will carefully guard what You have called and created me to do. I will multiply for Your glory every gift, skill, and opportunity You place in my hands. And I will eagerly look forward to the day when I stand in Your presence, because I want with all my heart to hear Your "Well done!" and receive Your reward and worship You forever.*

On that day, you will **prove** that you **valued** Jesus' **death** for you and you gave Him your **heart** and **life** in return.

The Jesus of the Last Page

In chapter 1, I showed you that the first thing Jesus talked about when He began to teach was that one day, God will reward those who serve Him. Now I want you to see that His amazing plan to reward you was the last thing He talked about too.

If you turn to the last page of Revelation, you will see what I mean. Here you'll read the final promise of Jesus:

> "Behold, I am coming quickly, and My reward is with Me, to give to every one according to his work."
>
> REVELATION 22:12

Notice that Jesus doesn't say, "I'm coming quickly to set up My kingdom." What He cares most about are the *people* of His kingdom—people who have given a lifetime to Him because they believed what He said, and they wanted to please Him, and they chose to be faithful.

People like you.

Never again doubt the truth. Jesus knows your heart. He notices and cares about your every attempt to serve Him. He promises to reward you...and He can't wait to do so!

Picture your homecoming, the moment when all of eternity and all the angels and saints pause for you. Heaven will hush as you stand before your Savior to hear Him say, "Well done, good and faithful servant!" And then heaven will erupt in a celebration as you receive the rewards of your life—the ones that Jesus is reserving just for you.

It will be your special moment to bless the heart of God. On that day, you will prove that you valued Jesus' death for you and you gave Him your heart and life in return.

God wants that day, when unseen and eternal things become visible, to be the most wonderful day of your life.

And I do too. This book is a gift to you for that day, with great anticipation.

BEHOLD I AM COMING QUICKLY A

Let's Talk about It

1. Up to now, has heaven been a place you don't think about much on a day-to-day basis? Why do you think this is so?

2. Do you believe that what Jesus revealed about His rewards could change your school, your church, maybe even the whole world? If so, what do you think your part could be?

3. How might making heaven your true "home" while you're on earth change the way you experience problems that come your way? How could it change your priorities? How could it make your life a lot happier and better?

4. Who in your life will be most affected by your new decision to live a life God rewards, and why?

5. What practical steps could you take right away to make sure that the message of this book continues to change the way you live? Who will you tell about your new commitment?

MY REWARD IS WITH ME

The BreakThrough Series, Book Three: *A Life God Rewards*™

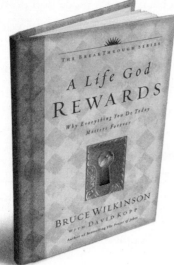

- ISBN 1-57673-976-7
- www.thebreakthroughseries.com

The BreakThrough Series,
Book One: *The Prayer of Jabez*™

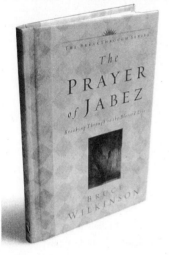

"Fastest selling book of all time."
  —Publishers Weekly

- ISBN 1-57673-733-0
- #1 *New York Times Bestseller*
- 11 Million in Print!
- www.prayerofjabez.com
- www.thebreakthroughseries.com
- 2001& 2002 Gold Medallion Book of the Year

• The Prayer of Jabez Audio	ISBN 1-57673-842-6
• The Prayer of Jabez Audio CD	ISBN 1-57673-907-4
• The Prayer of Jabez for Women	ISBN 1-57673-962-7
• The Prayer of Jabez for Women Audio	ISBN 1-57673-963-5
• The Prayer of Jabez Leather Edition	ISBN 1-57673-857-4
• The Prayer of Jabez Journal	ISBN 1-57673-860-4
• The Prayer of Jabez Devotional	ISBN 1-57673-844-2
• The Prayer of Jabez Bible Study	ISBN 1-57673-979-1
• The Prayer of Jabez Bible Study: Leader's Edition	
	ISBN 1-57673-980-5
• The Prayer of Jabez for Teens	ISBN 1-57673-815-9
• The Prayer of Jabez for Teens Audio CD	ISBN 1-57673-904-X
• The Prayer of Jabez Gift Edition	ISBN 1-57673-810-8

The BreakThrough Series, Book Two: *Secrets of the Vine*™

#2 New York Times Bestseller

- ISBN 1-57673-975-9
- Over 3 Million in Print!
- www.thebreakthroughseries.com

• **Secrets of the Vine Audio Cassette**	ISBN 1-57673-977-5
• **Secrets of the Vine Audio CD**	ISBN 1-57673-908-2
• **Secrets of the Vine Leather Edition**	ISBN 1-57673-876-0
• **Secrets of the Vine Journal**	ISBN 1-57673-960-0
• **Secrets of the Vine Devotional**	ISBN 1-57673-959-7
• **Secrets of the Vine Bible Study**	ISBN 1-57673-972-4
• **Secrets of the Vine Bible Study: Leader's Edition**	
	ISBN 1-57673-973-2
• **Secrets of the Vine Gift Edition**	ISBN 1-57673-915-5
• **Secrets of the Vine for Teens**	ISBN 1-57673-922-8
• **Secrets of the Vine for Teens Audio CD**	ISBN 1-59052-111-0